TECH BYTES

EXPLORING SPACE

BLACK HOLES

BY JOEL GREEN

NORWOOD HOUSE PRESS

NORWOOD HOUSE PRESS

Cover: A NASA illustration of what a black hole might look like

For more information about Norwood House Press, please visit our website at: www.norwoodhousepress.com or call 866-565-2900.

Book Designer: Ed Morgan
Editorial and Production: Bowerbird Books

Photo Credits: NASA's Goddard Space Flight Center/CI Lab, cover; Event Horizon Telescope, title page; ESO/O. Furtak, 4; freepik.com, 5; Event Horizon Telescope Collaboration, 5 right; freepik.com, 6; ESO/L. Calçada/M.Kornmesser, 7; AIP Emilio Segrè Visual Archives, Gift of Kameshwar Wali., 8; Wikimedia Commons/Alain r, 9; Wikimedia Commons/Roger W Haworth, 10; ESA/Hubble, 11; X-ray: NASA/CXC and Optical: Digitized Sky Survey, 12–13; X-ray: NASA/UMass/D.Wang et al., IR: NASA/STScI, 14; NASA, 15; NASA, ESA, and D. Coe, J. Anderson, and R. van der Marel (STScI), 16; freepik.com, 17; NASA, 18; Wikimedia Commons/Brandon Defrise Carter (presumed)/Event Horizon Telescope, 19; © Dirk Gillissen, 20 top; NASA, 20 bottom; NASA/ESA/STScI, 21; EHT collaboration (acknowledgment: Lia Medeiros, xkcd), 22; Public Domain, 23; Wikimedia Commons/Laura A. Whitlock, Kara C. Granger, Jane D. Mahon, 24–25; NASA, 26; © ESA–D. Ducros, 2013, 27; Wikimedia Commons/ SiOwl, 28; NASA/MSFC/David Higginbotham, 29; W.M. Keck Observatory, 30; NASA, 31; freepik.com, 32; NASA/JPL-Caltech, 33; Event Horizon Telescope Collaboration, 34; ESO/M. Kornmesser, 35; freepik.com, 36; Hubble/European Space Agency, 37; NASA Goddard Space Flight Center/ Chris Gunn from Greenbelt, MD, USA, 38; Event Horizon Telescope Collaboration, 39; NASA; 40; NASA, 41; Event Horizon Telescope, 42–42.

Hardcover ISBN: 978-1-68450-731-3
Paperback ISBN: 978-1-68404-835-9

Library of Congress Cataloging-in-Publication Data has been filed and is available at catalog.loc.gov

359N—012023

Manufactured in the United States of America in North Mankato, Minnesota.

CONTENTS

Words that are bolded in the text are defined in the glossary.

CHAPTER 1
BLACK HOLE DISCOVERY

The most mysterious objects in our universe are black holes. Some are smaller than the Sun. Others are bigger than millions of Suns combined. Black holes slowly grow larger by feeding on other things in space that get too close to them, such as interstellar dust, gas, or even entire stars! Once black holes have something within their powerful field of gravity, they don't let go. Yet scientists have never actually seen a black hole. Sera Markoff, a Professor of astrophysics at the University of Amsterdam in the Netherlands, was part of a team that wanted to change that.

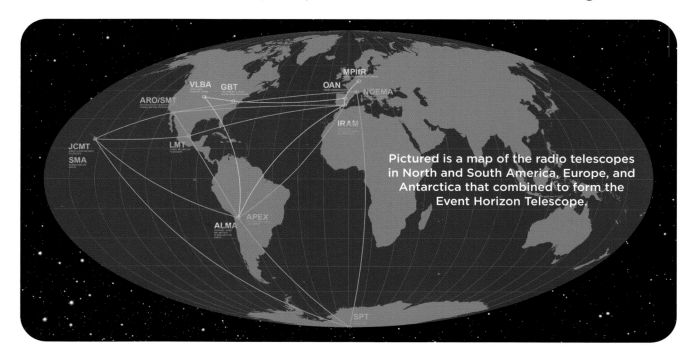

Pictured is a map of the radio telescopes in North and South America, Europe, and Antarctica that combined to form the Event Horizon Telescope.

Using cutting-edge technology, Markoff and a group of scientists from around the world built a telescope to see what a real black hole looks like. More precisely, they put together one massive telescope—the Event Horizon Telescope—by combining lots of smaller telescopes known as radio dish telescopes. Each of these little telescopes took its own picture. Once assembled with the other dish telescope images, they would create the first image of a black hole! In 2017, these telescopes peered at the swirling star-filled center of a galaxy called Messier 87. On April 10, 2019, Markoff and the other scientists were ready to share some exciting findings with the world—the very first picture of a black hole!

DID YOU KNOW?

Sera Markoff plays an important role on the Event Horizon Team. However, the team has more than 200 scientists and engineers from 20 different countries working together toward the common goal of science!

The Event Horizon team

WHAT is GRAVITY?

As early as 1665, the mathematician Isaac Newton wondered about the force that pulls apples from a tree in his yard to the ground. He figured out that gravity makes all things fall back to Earth. Eventually, scientists realized that *everything*, not just Earth, has gravity. It is a force in the universe that pulls all things toward everything else, including planets, moons, and other objects in space. Gravity gets stronger as objects get closer to each other and are more massive. Earth's gravity is not very strong. Despite Earth's large size and gravitational pull, people can still jump into the air, for example. Also, the Sun has enough gravity to keep Earth orbiting around it but not enough to pull the planet inside it.

Why don't buildings collapse if gravity pulls them down to Earth? The answer is structure and support. Just like buildings have supports, our bodies have bones and muscles that keep us upright.

An image showing what gravity pulling a star towards a black hole might look like

As scientists continued to think about gravity, they began to wonder about stars much more massive than the Sun. Could a star get so dense that gravity would cause it to collapse from the inside out? Also, once a star starts to collapse, would its gravity get stronger and cause it to collapse faster? In 1784, scientist John Michell wondered if a star could get so massive that even light could not escape its gravity.

The EXISTENCE of BLACK HOLES

In 1915, scientist Albert Einstein was trying to figure out how the world and gravity work. He was developing a theory called relativity that improved on Isaac Newton's theory. The relativity theory describes how everything in the universe is affected by gravity, including objects in space. Another scientist, Karl Schwarzschild, figured out how gravity from a super-dense single point—known as a singularity (sing-gyuh-LAIR-ih-tee)—would work in Einstein's new theory. He discovered that if a star started to collapse, there would be a point where nothing could stop or escape it. At that point, not even light was fast enough to escape the pull of gravity. A few years later in 1931, another scientist named Subrahmanyan Chandrasekhar calculated that a dense star core with more mass than that of our Sun could collapse to a tiny point. By the 1960s, scientists had named these points black holes. However, did black holes actually exist?

Subrahmanyan Chandrasekhar

While Einstein was figuring out how gravity worked, astronomers were trying to understand the night sky. They knew that Earth was one of eight planets orbiting a star called the Sun. They also knew that Earth was round and spinning. They were pretty sure the Sun and other stars had been shining for a very long time. Yet they didn't know that the Sun would continue shining for billions of years, burning fuel in its core. They didn't know that all the stars our eyes can see are part of a single galaxy called the Milky Way, one of billions of galaxies in the universe. They didn't yet know that the most massive stars would explode, leaving behind black holes.

THE UNIVERSE IN EINSTEIN'S DAY

This is an artist's sketch of a black hole and the effect of its gravity on passing light from stars behind it.

HUNTING for BLACK HOLES

To prove Chandrasekhar's theory, scientists would need to find a massive star core. Astronomers went looking for signs of very dense objects in space. In 1967, using a radio telescope in a farm field in England, astronomer Jocelyn Bell Burnell discovered something new in the night sky. She found a tiny object that was spinning so rapidly that unless it was very, very dense would fly apart. Burnell determined that the object wasn't dense enough to be a black hole, but it was a lot denser than anything else astronomers had ever found! She had discovered a neutron star. Neutron stars form from the core of a dying star bigger than our Sun. They are as heavy as our Sun, but they are still only about as big as New York City. Also, light and particles can still escape neutron stars, meaning they are not dense enough to be black holes. So where could a true black hole be found?

Jocelyn Bell Burnell in 1967, when she discovered the first neutron star

THE DENSEST THINGS IN THE UNIVERSE

The cores of stars are extremely dense. How dense are they? Our bodies are mostly made of water. Water has a density of 1 gram per cubic centimeter (g/cc). The Sun is mostly made of hot gas and is not very dense either, only 1.4 g/cc. Earth is mainly made of rocks, iron, and water, and has a density of about 5.5 g/cc. When our Sun runs out of fuel in 5 billion years, its core will collapse to form a white dwarf star. This type of star is a million times denser than the Sun. Other than small black holes, neutron stars are the densest objects in the universe. They're 100 million times denser than white dwarfs. It is not known how dense black holes are. A black hole as massive as the Sun would be at least 100 times denser than a neutron star! But the bigger a black hole is, the less dense it becomes.

This is a neutron star in the middle of the Crab Nebula. The Crab Nebula is the shattered remains of an exploded star.

FINDING the FIRST BLACK HOLE

Light comes in different forms. Some forms are visible and others, like X-rays, are invisible. X-rays are not just for checking if a bone is broken. These very powerful rays of light also come from objects in space. To detect X-rays in space, astronomers use a special instrument called an X-ray telescope. In 1962, they put an X-ray telescope on a rocket and launched it out of Earth's atmosphere. They wanted to see the X-rays coming from a mysterious pair of stars called Cygnus X-1. (The "X" in Cygnus X-1 stands for X-ray.) The telescope picked up a large bright star and a dark heavy object. The gravity of each object pulled on the other. Scientists used this information to calculate how much each object weighed. The dark object was more than twice the mass of our Sun—and heavier than Jocelyn Bell Burnell's neutron star. By 1975, astronomers believed the dark object was a black hole! Cygnus X-1 was the first direct evidence of a black hole. Astronomers wanted to know more, including whether there was a black hole at the center of our very own galaxy.

This two-part illustration shows a distant (left) and close-up (right) image of the star Cygnus X-1.

DID YOU KNOW?

Humans travel to space, but most missions to space are performed by machines, including rockets, telescopes, and robots such as rovers. Sending machines to space is cheaper and safer than sending humans. Plus, machines can withstand the harsh conditions in space, like extreme temperatures and high radiation levels.

In the 1970s, astronomers Bruce Balick and Robert Brown used a radio telescope to look at the center of our galaxy. They found a huge amount of material packed into a tiny space smaller than our solar system. This region became known as Sagittarius A* (pronounced A-star). Starting in the 1980s, astronomers measured the gravity of Sagittarius A* by seeing how the nearby stars moved around it. They discovered something amazing. In 2008, scientists Reinhard Gentzel and Andrea Ghez used the space-based Chandra X-ray Observatory to discover that Sagittarius A* weighed as much as four million

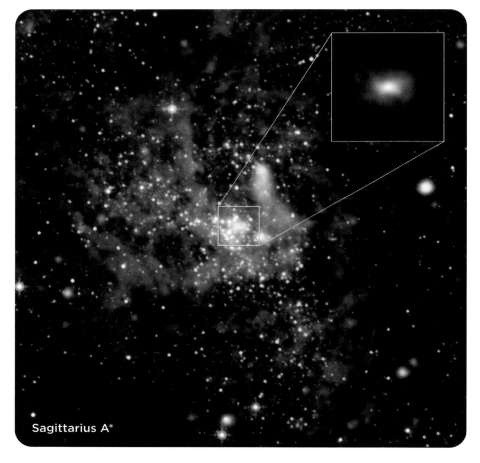

Sagittarius A*

Suns! It had to be a black hole—what else could fit into such a tight space? In addition, this black hole was in the middle of our galaxy! Sagittarius A* was much, much bigger than scientists like Einstein and Chandrasekhar had ever imagined.

THE CHANDRA X-RAY OBSERVATORY

The Chandra X-ray Observatory is named after Subrahmanyan Chandrasekhar. A high school teacher and student came up with its name as part of a NASA (National Aeronautics and Space Administration) contest. NASA is a U.S. government organization founded in 1957 to explore space. The Chandra X-ray Observatory is a sophisticated telescope that picks up X-rays from very hot parts of the universe, such as exploded stars and matter around black holes. It was launched into space by the Space Shuttle Columbia in 1999 and is still operating as of today.

An image of the Chandra X-ray Observatory

CHAPTER 2
WHAT ARE BLACK HOLES?

After decades of learning about black holes, scientists now have a better understanding of what they are. So why are black holes different from stars and other things in space? What makes black holes incredibly special is their gravity. Black holes that are similar to the Sun's mass pack more mass per square inch than anything else in the universe! These types of black holes are very small. They're so small that it's not easy for them to trap interstellar dust or other particles to grow bigger. These particles have to get very close to a black hole in order to be captured. Interestingly, the more massive a black hole is, the bigger it gets. Supermassive black holes—those containing millions of Suns in mass—are less dense than water.

The edge of a black hole is the location of the strongest gravity in the universe. It's called the event horizon. The pull of gravity is so strong here that even light—the fastest thing in the universe—can't escape. The absence of light makes a black hole look like a dark void in space, which is how it earned its name.

This is a computer-generated picture of a black hole at the center of a galaxy bending the light and matter around it.

GRAVITY
IN SPACE

This diagram shows the order of the planets in the solar system. The Sun (at left) has the strongest gravity.

On Earth, we think of gravity as a force that pulls us downward. Outer space appears empty of everything, including gravity. However, space isn't empty—it is full of stuff! The Sun, planets, asteroids, and dust particles all swirl around. Each of these things has gravity—the bigger the object, the more gravity. Gravity gets stronger the closer you get to the source.

ARE ALL BLACK HOLES the SAME?

Like humans, all the stars in the universe are unique. They form in different places from various materials. Some stars contain more of certain elements. Other stars have many planets around them. Stars are also different ages, which can affect their size. Planets are unique too. Some have rocky surfaces, while others are mostly made of gas. There are planets covered with ice, water, deserts, and bubbling lava. In the 1970s, physicist Stephen Hawking proposed that black holes are almost identical—unlike stars and planets. He said the only difference between black holes is how much they weigh, how fast they spin, and whether they have an electric charge.

Physicist Stephen Hawking

A model of a black hole

Could this theory be correct? Two humans that weigh the same can still be different, right? However, scientists think that two black holes that weigh the same would look exactly the same and be the same size. If scientists switched them like two playing cards, they wouldn't be able to tell which one was which. Or would they? What is true of all black holes is that anything that falls inside is gone forever. The black hole gains mass equal to whatever falls inside it, but the lost object can never be recovered or reconstructed. The object would totally merge with the black hole and lose all of its characteristics.

Physicist John Wheeler supported this theory and wrote that "black holes have no hair." He meant that all black holes look the same. However, scientists like Sera Markoff are hard at work proving him wrong by "putting the hair on black holes." This is why Markoff wanted to take the first picture of a black

Sera Markoff

hole—to observe the area just outside of it and see if there are differences. Black holes are very dark and hard to see, but they can be identified by how they affect everything around them. Sometimes, they are paired with a single star and draw material from it in a stream.

This is an artist's idea of what a black hole pulling material from a nearby star into a disk around itself might look like.

Material that falls into black holes doesn't fall in directly. Occasionally, the stream ends up turning into a flat, funnel-shaped disk. This disk surrounds the black hole, spinning like the rings of Saturn, but on a much larger scale. Other times, the material from the disk gets thrown out instead of being pulled in. This material leaves the area at high speeds, usually in the form of a jet. Think of water shooting out of a fountain. However, in a black hole, the material shoots out both ends equally! This keeps the black hole balanced in the middle. The jets can be "about a billion times larger than the black hole event horizon that launches them," says Markoff.

This image shows huge jets emerging from a black hole in the center of the Hercules A galaxy.

BLACK HOLE SIZE

Scientists can learn more about black holes by measuring their event horizons. This helps them determine a black hole's size. The size of the event horizon depends on the black hole's mass. The least-heavy black holes are about the mass of our Sun. Yet their event horizon is much, much smaller than our Sun. However, black holes can also be a lot bigger. The black hole in the center of Messier 87 is several billion Suns in mass. It is more than four times bigger than our entire Solar System—or about 24 billion miles (38.6 billion km) across! Consider packing a few billion Suns into a space only a little bigger than our solar system.

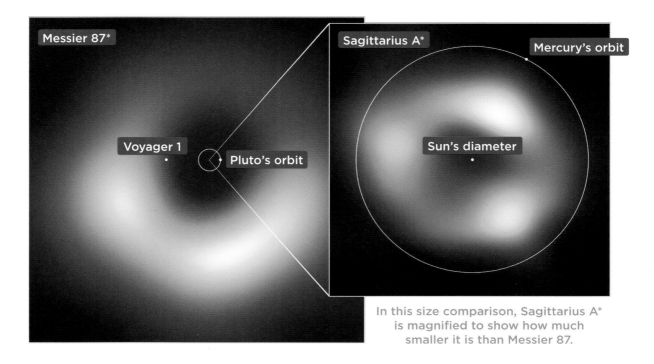

Messier 87*

Voyager 1

Pluto's orbit

Sagittarius A*

Mercury's orbit

Sun's diameter

In this size comparison, Sagittarius A* is magnified to show how much smaller it is than Messier 87.

THE **POINT** OF NO RETURN

Another name for the event horizon—or point of no return—of a black hole is the Schwarzschild radius. It was named after a German scientist, Karl Schwarzschild. He figured out the precise distance from the center of a black hole to the event horizon. Like a horizon on Earth where the surface and sky appear to meet, nothing can be seen beyond it. This is why it's called the point of no return.

Karl Schwarzschild

INSIDE A
BLACK HOLE

So what's inside a black hole? The nearest black hole is very far away. Because scientists understand how black holes work, they can imagine what falling into one might be like, but no one will ever know for sure. It's a one-way trip—anything that gets pulled into a black hole never comes out!

Let's say a person fell into a black hole. What would happen? The answer is all about perspective. For example, imagine two people are flying on a spaceship near a black hole and one falls in. The middle of a black hole is thought to be a singularity—a place where all the mass of a black hole is crushed together. The person's body would be pulled toward that spot, gently at first, and then faster and faster. This means that their body would gradually stretch, becoming long and skinny. This is called spaghettification. After some time, the person would completely disappear. The person in the spaceship would see things very differently. They would see the other person appear to slow down while approaching the black hole. This is because the gravity of black holes is so strong that it bends space and time. Everything that has mass can bend space and time a little. Black holes can bend space and time much more because they have so much mass.

A diagram showing spaghettification

CHAPTER 3
STUDYING BLACK HOLES

Think about how many stars are visible in the sky on a dark, clear night. In the darkest areas on Earth with the fewest lights shining, a person with good eyesight might spot several thousand stars. However, this is only a tiny fraction of all the stars in the sky. Most stars are too faint to be seen with the naked eye because they are so far away. Also, many stars are obscured by interstellar dust. Scientists use telescope technology to better see and study the stars. For example, Gaia is a space telescope, or observatory, launched by the European Space Agency (ESA) in 2013. Gaia's mission is to measure the positions, distances, and motion of the stars. So far, Gaia has taken the measurements of more than 1.8 billion stars and is still counting! Telescopes are incredibly important to modern astronomy and the study of black holes because they allow scientists to collect large amounts of light with much greater precision than a human eye.

This is a combined set of 400 pictures taken by the Hubble Space Telescope of a section of the Andromeda Galaxy. There are 100 million stars in this picture.

Gaia's goal is to create the largest three-dimensional map of our galaxy, the Milky Way. The 4,473-pound (2,029-kg) telescope carries special instruments that can measure the motion of each star in its orbit around the center of the galaxy. Gaia will also observe the same stars—an average of 70 times—over several years to capture their precise brightness, positions, and movement. In addition to mapping the stars, Gaia will study asteroids within the solar system.

GAIA STATS

This is an illustration of the Gaia Space Observatory.

TELESCOPES as TOOLS

Telescopes are better than human eyes in several ways, including in their ability to detect different amounts of light. A person collects light through the pupil in their eye. The pupil is a dark, circular opening in the center of the eye that lets light inside. In dark conditions, the pupil becomes wider to let in more light. Telescopes have holes called apertures that function like pupils. Telescopes also use mirrors to bounce as much light as possible into a small processing area.

The W.M. Keck Observatory is located on Mauna Kea, a mountain in Hawaii. It has two of the largest telescopes in the world.

Telescope mirrors are manufactured to be perfectly curved. They focus light in a very small space. This means that they can be pointed at a distant object in space and collect the maximum amount of light. For example, NASA's James Webb Space Telescope has eighteen mirrors. Each mirror is so smooth that if it were stretched out across the entire United States, the biggest bumps on it will only be a few inches tall! Larger telescopes have bigger mirrors and, consequently, higher resolution. They can capture the most detailed images of space.

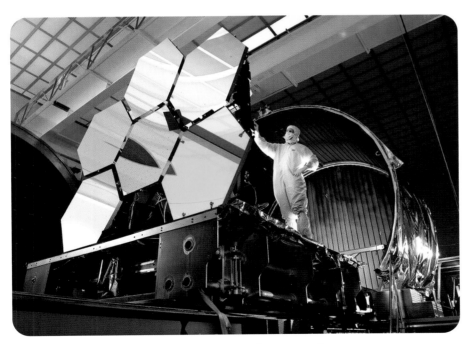

James Webb Space Telescope mirrors

day

night

DID YOU KNOW?

The width of a human pupil is about 0.07–0.15 inches (2–4 mm) during the day and twice that at night. One of the W.M. Keck Observatory's telescopes in Hawaii has a mirror that is 32.8 feet (10 m) across! That's an "eye" as big as a small school bus!

Telescopes can also help people see things in space with greater clarity. Did you know that there is some truth in the children's poem and song, *Twinkle, Twinkle Little Star*? Twinkling is an effect of Earth's atmosphere that causes light to flicker as it passes from space to Earth. This phenomenon distorts the way stars look and makes them appear fuzzy. Telescopes can adjust for this in one of two ways. For example, each of the Keck telescopes uses a special technique called adaptive optics to allow the mirror to bend and flex. Keck's mirror is made up of many smaller mirrors. For every picture Keck takes, each mirror flexes itself many times per second in response to the atmosphere. The mirror can also be adjusted with computer software.

This is a photo of the Keck telescope's large mirror made from smaller hexagonal (6-sided) mirrors pieced together like a jigsaw puzzle.

This photo shows the space shuttle Discovery on its launchpad. The Hubble Space Telescope is packed inside the shuttle in a cargo-holding area called the payload bay.

In contrast, the Hubble Space Telescope avoids the atmosphere altogether. It orbits in space where there is no atmosphere to distort anything! Although Hubble's mirror is much smaller than Keck's set of mirrors, Hubble can see even fainter objects in space.

DID YOU KNOW?

The Hubble Space Telescope was launched on April 24, 1990, on the space shuttle Discovery. Hubble has been serviced and upgraded by astronauts five times—in 1993, 1997, 1999, 2002, and 2009.

TYPES of LIGHT

Advanced telescope technology can also pick up different kinds of light. Human eyes can only see visible light in the form of the colors of the rainbow. Yet there are many other kinds of light that people can't see! Infrared light is redder than visible red light and can sometimes be felt as heat from the Sun. Ultraviolet light can give people sunburn. X-ray light is even more powerful, but Earth's atmosphere protects us from it. Radio waves are harmless to people and can pass through almost anything. Radio waves are even "redder" than infrared light and are used to send signals in space. Microwaves and gamma rays are also different kinds of light. All of these light types also come from space objects. Each can be detected by a different kind of telescope. These specialized machines then use that information to make computer images for people to see in regular color. Each type of light provides scientists with different information about space—and about black holes.

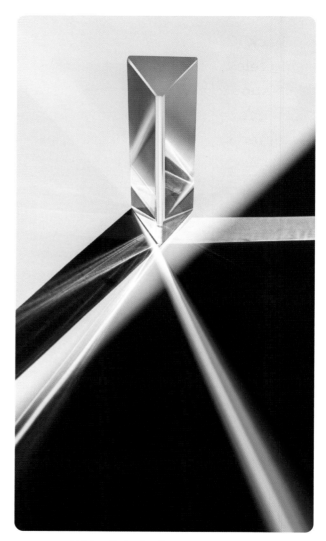

White light is dispersed through a spectrum into light people can see.

Black holes are dark in visible light, but their edges are very bright in radio wave light. Using telescopes available at the time, the black hole in Messier 87 looked like a bright radio spot to astronomers. Sera Markoff and the team knew that if they could make a radio telescope large enough, they could see the details of the blurry dot. Einstein and others predicted how big a black hole would be, and Markoff could finally test that theory.

This illustration shows reddish infrared light coming from a star that's being devoured by a black hole.

DID YOU KNOW?

Everything that gets close to a black hole gets redder and redder. When things get extremely close to a black hole, they pass beyond "red," and eventually become radio waves!

BLACK HOLE IMAGE

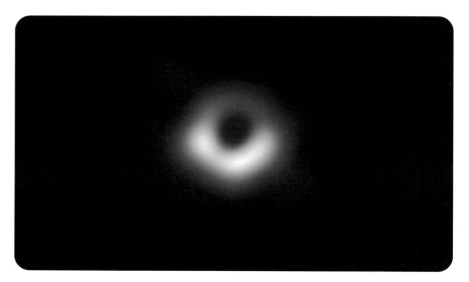

This is the first direct picture of a black hole ever taken.

On April 10, 2019, a news conference was held in six different cities around the globe: Brussels, Santiago, Shanghai, Taipei, Tokyo, and Washington, D.C. Sera Markoff traveled from Amsterdam to Washington, D.C., to share the team's findings with the entire world. She gathered with other scientists, including Shep Doeleman, leader of the Event Horizon Telescope at the Harvard/Smithsonian Center. As the lights dimmed, everyone looked at the big screen above the scientists' heads. Markoff and the others presented the very first picture of a black hole at the heart of the galaxy Messier 87. The image showed a lopsided ring surrounding a dark center. People gasped, cheered, and clapped enthusiastically. "We have seen what we thought was unseeable," said Doeleman. The image was the result of two years of computers analyzing the observations of the Event Horizon Telescope, as well as the hard work of Markoff, Doeleman, and the other scientists involved.

The Event Horizon Telescope is made up of smaller radio telescopes that are coordinated to capture an image of a black hole. The telescopes are spread out across Earth. They are located in the United States and Hawaii, Mexico, Spain, France, Greenland, and Chile. The telescopes use radio light to take the best picture of material around a black hole's event horizon.

THE EVENT HORIZON TELESCOPE

A composite image showing the many Event Horizon telescopes

CHAPTER 4
FUTURE EXPLORATION

What does the future hold for black hole exploration? The Event Horizon telescope team is adding more telescopes to the Event Horizon network to gather data. In addition, scientists are using other types of telescopes to learn even more about black holes. One is the Chandra Observatory, which examines high-energy jets shooting from black holes. Chandra can help scientists figure out how much material in space black holes are gobbling up.

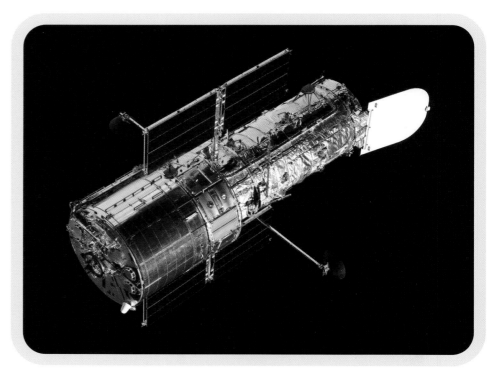

The Hubble Space Telescope

Scientists are also using the Hubble Space Telescope to take detailed pictures of the stars around black holes. The Hubble is a visible light telescope that takes amazingly precise pictures of the stars. Hubble accurately measures the stars' movement, essentially tracing their paths. These star paths reveal how much gravity a black hole has, and, therefore, its weight, helping scientists gain further knowledge about black holes.

This image of deep space was taken by the Hubble.

DID YOU KNOW?

The Hubble Space Telescope orbits at a speed of over 17,000 miles (27,358 km) per hour, more than 300 miles (482 km) above Earth. The European Space Agency (ESA) and the Canadian Space Agency (CSA) work together with NASA on the Hubble space telescope project.

In 2021, the largest, most powerful space telescope ever built was launched into space. The James Webb Space Telescope is as tall as a three-story building and stretches the length of a tennis court. It's so big that it had to be folded up on the rocket when it was carried into space! The Webb telescope is using its infrared cameras to peer through the interstellar dust in the universe, allowing scientists to see where new stars and planets are forming. It is capturing images of some of the first galaxies, as well as searching for the first black holes to form in the universe. Webb may also be able to see the disks and jets around these original black holes because their light has been stretched into infrared light.

The James Webb Space Telescope

A FUZZY DONUT

The black hole in Messier 87 looks like a fuzzy doughnut. The size and shape of the "doughnut" match what Einstein and others predicted a hundred years earlier. The doughnut looks small because it is so far away—55 million light years. However, the black hole's event horizon is 24 billion miles (38.6 billion km) across. That means that stars have to stay far away from it to avoid being torn up and pulled into it.

A view of the Messier 87 supermassive black hole

COLLIDING BLACK HOLES

Scientists have also developed a technology called laser interferometers to investigate black holes. When two black holes get too close, they eventually join together to form a bigger black hole. When they merge, they release a big ripple called a gravitational wave that rolls out across the universe, like the ripples from a big rock thrown into a pond. Laser interferometers detect these ripples in space and time.

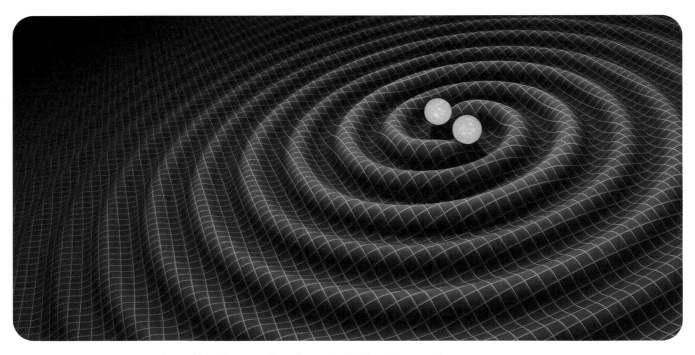

An artist's image showing gravitational waves in space

One kind called LIGO uses two different instruments placed in Washington and Louisiana in the United States, and, since 2017, a third in Pisa, Italy. Another interferometer called LISA will be launched into space by the European Space Agency (ESA). LISA will be able to detect new types of objects, including black holes, that even LIGO cannot see.

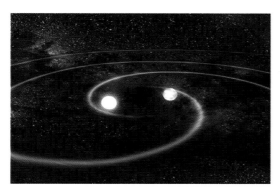

These pictures show neutron stars colliding

DID YOU KNOW?

Gravitational waves are surprisingly common. This means that a lot of black holes are merging. Not all gravitational waves come from two black holes merging, though. Two neutron stars can also combine to make a black hole and cause ripples.

ANOTHER BLACK HOLE PICTURE

What's better than one picture of a black hole? A second image of a black hole! After Messier 87, the Event Horizon Telescope focused on Sagittarius A* at the center of our own Milky Way galaxy. Sagittarius A* is a thousand times less massive than the one at the center of Messier 87. The incredible picture was released in April 2022. Sagittarius A* looks a lot like Messier 87's black hole. This is because the same theories apply to both black holes. However, Sagittarius A* is also a thousand times closer, so it looks similar even though it is much smaller. Scientists plan to compare the two images and take new pictures of other black holes. "Two very different black holes like Sagittarius A* and Messier 87 will bend light around themselves in the same way," explains Markoff.

Scientists will also use new telescopes like the James Webb Space Telescope to understand how black holes form and grow. They plan to build newer and bigger telescopes to increase the detail of these pictures. Astrophysicists like Markoff still have many questions about black holes: Do all galaxies have big black holes in their centers? Can black holes grow on their own, or do the big ones form during collisions with other galaxies? There are many more astonishing discoveries about black holes yet to be made.

This is a picture of the black hole in the center of our Milky Way galaxy, called Sagittarius A*, taken by the Event Horizon Telescope in 2022. TV shows like *Interstellar* and *Star Trek* are already showing pictures of black holes that are based on the real ones!

DID YOU KNOW?

Some scientists like Stephen Hawking have proposed that microscopic—smaller than a single cell—black holes could exist, but no evidence has yet been found to support this theory.

GLOSSARY

apertures (AP-er-cherz): openings that allow or limit light to enter instruments like telescopes.

asteroids (AS-tuh-roid): large and small rocky space objects that revolve around the Sun.

astronauts (ASS-truh-nawts): people who travel into space.

astrophysics (as-troh-FIZ-iks): the study of the universe and stars and planets.

atmosphere (AT-muhss-fihr): the mixture of gases and particles surrounding a planet.

calculated (KAL-kyuh-ley-tid): figured out using math.

clarity (KLAR-ih-tee): clear or transparent to the eye.

dense (DENSS): having a high mass in a small space.

evidence (EV-uh-duhnss): information or facts that support an argument.

galaxy (GAL-uhk-see): a large group of millions or billions of stars, gas, and dust held together by gravity.

gravity (GRAV-uh-tee): the force that pulls things with mass towards each other.

infrared light (in-fruh-RED LYT): light that is invisible to the human eye and often comes from warm objects.

interferometers (in-ter-fuh-ROM-ih-terz): science instruments that work together to make one precise measurement using the wave properties of light.

interstellar dust (in-ter-STEL-er DUHST): solid particles in space.

mass (MASS): the amount of matter in an object; mass never changes while weight varies according to the strength of gravity.

massive (MASS-iv): large, or containing a lot of mass.

neutron star (NOO-tron STAHR): a dense, small star, usually formed from the core of a dying star.

obscured (uhb-SKYOORD): concealed or hard to see.

orbiting (OR-bit-ing): moving around something in a continuous loop.

perspective (per-SPEK-tiv): point of view.

phenomenon (fuh-NOM-uh-non): an action or event.

physicist (FIZ-uh-sist): a scientist who studies matter and energy.

radiation (ray-dee-AY-shuhn): light that carries energy out of particles.

radio dish telescopes (REY-dee-oh DISH TEL-uh-skohpz): tools shaped like big dishes that collect radio signals that are turned into visual images.

resolution (rez-uh-LOO-shuhn): the degree of detail in an image.

rovers (ROH-verz): vehicles that explore other planets.

telescope (TEL-uh-skohp): a tool for collecting light and sensing distant objects in great detail.

theory (THIHR-ee): a set of mathematical rules that are consistent with all facts and evidence.

FOR MORE INFORMATION

Books

Aguilar, David A. *Space Encyclopedia*. Washington, DC: National Geographic, 2020.
Tour the solar system and beyond in this comprehensive book on space exploration.

Anderson, Amy, and Brian Anderson. *Space Dictionary for Kids*. New York, NY: Routledge, 2016.
Learn all about rockets, astronauts, the universe, and the fascinating world of space exploration.

DeGrasse Tyson, Neil. *Astrophysics for Young People in a Hurry*. New York, NY: Norton Young Readers, 2019.
Read about the mysteries of the universe in this accessible and exciting book.

Koontz, Robin. *Our Place in Space*. Vero Beach, FL: Rourke Educational Media, 2016.
Explore Earth's place in the universe and learn space-related facts.

Websites

NASA Kids' Club (https://www.nasa.gov/kidsclub/index.html)
NASA provides an online place for children to play as they learn about NASA and its missions.

NASA Science Space Place (https://spaceplace.nasa.gov)
NASA's award-winning Space Place website engages children in space and Earth science through interactive games, hands-on activities, and more.

National Geographic Kids—Facts About Mars (https://www.natgeokids.com/uk/discover/science/space/facts-about-mars/)
Young readers will uncover cool facts about the Red Planet.

National Geographic Kids—History of Space Travel (https://kids.nationalgeographic.com/space/article/history-of-space-travel)
Learn about the history of humans traveling into space.

Space Center Houston (https://spacecenter.org/exhibits-and-experiences/journey-to-space/)
Space Center Houston is a leading science and space exploration learning center.

Places to Visit
Kennedy Space Center in Merritt Island, FL
(https://www.kennedyspacecenter.com/?utm_source=google&utm_medium=yext)
NASA's Kennedy Space Center features exhibits and historic spacecraft and memorabilia.

The National Air and Space Museum in Washington, DC
(https://www.si.edu/museums/air-and-space-museum)
The National Air and Space Museum maintains the world's largest and most significant collection of aviation and space artifacts.

Rose Center for Earth and Space in New York, NY
(https://www.amnh.org/exhibitions/permanent/rose-center)
Explore the cosmos, the history of the universe, galaxies, Earth, and more at the Rose Center at the American Museum for Natural History.

INDEX

ABOUT THE AUTHOR

Joel Green is an astrophysicist and an instrument scientist working on the Hubble Space Telescope. He studies how stars and planets are born and wants to understand Earth's place in the cosmos. He lives in the farm fields near Baltimore and hopes for clear nights and dark skies.